DYNAMIC
BUSINESS PLANNING
BASICS

DYNAMIC BUSINESS PLANNING BASICS

An Adaptable Planning Process for Disruptive Times

Carol L. Fatuzzo
and
Ennio Fatuzzo

PREFACE

This book, "**_Dynamic Business Planning Basics_**", is a guide to a business planning process that is appropriate for use in disruptive economic times such as ours. It is not meant to be a comprehensive treatise on business plans. Instead, it focuses on the planning **PROCESS** itself, not the written plan. It teaches a simple, seven-step planning methodology for building a strong business plan framework and then outlines an approach for using this methodology to create a "**_Living Business Plan_**".

What is a living business plan? It is a dynamic but simple document customized for a particular business. It is specific enough to provide a roadmap that can be followed, but not so complex that those using it get lost in the details. It is a plan with adaptability built into the process for maintaining it in order to allow for rapid changes in course as roadblocks are encountered in today's changing world.

Who needs another business planning book? Think about it. Is your business healthy? Are you satisfied with the results in these difficult economic times? Are you keeping pace with your competitors? Is your business adaptable to the changing environment?

We don't have all of the answers, but we do provide new insights into an "old" topic that we hope will stimulate new directions for business survival and growth in today's environment.

CONTENTS

DYNAMIC BUSINESS PLANNING BASICS

An Adaptable Planning Process
for Disruptive Times

INTRODUCTION

DYNAMIC BUSINESS PLANNING

What is "Dynamic Business Planning"? This is our term for a seven-step process that provides the adaptive framework necessary for business survival in a changing environment. It is a business planning process that focuses on defining clear goals and strategies and developing specific action plans to attain them. But it is more than that.

To develop the most useful "roadmap" for a specific business situation, Dynamic Business Planning incorporates what we call the "4 Rs":

- Realism. For your business plan to lead to success, you must have a realistic picture of both your internal world (your company, your business) and the external environment (competition, technology advances, and other external forces beyond your control). To create such a picture, our process includes methodologies for realistic assessments of your business, the industry/markets in which you participate, and your current plans.

- <u>Risk.</u> All plans and actions involve some degree of risk, and the rewards also vary. We provide techniques for evaluating these risks versus the potential rewards. Our focus is primarily on new markets, new businesses, and new programs, but the tools suggested are appropriate for assessing existing business elements as well. However, only you can decide what the right balance of risk/reward is for your business situation because only you know your "risk tolerance".

- <u>Resources.</u> Because resource requirements and timing are often underestimated, our planning process places emphasis on these areas – in setting goals, in determining strategies, and in developing action plans.

- <u>Redirection.</u> And finally, if a business plan is not a *living* document, it will soon be obsolete. It becomes an out-of-date "roadmap" that doesn't accurately take into account new roads and detours. Such unexpected changes can and do occur suddenly and frequently. Therefore our dynamic planning process includes suggestions for a review system that identifies red flags and helps you determine appropriate mid-course corrections – to programs or to the plan itself.

THE RATIONALE

To understand the rationale behind the dynamic planning process, think about sailing. When you navigate calm seas, you can reach your destination by relying on your experience and directions from the stars – even if your ship is old and fragile. However, in stormy and foggy weather, your ship had better be seaworthy. And you need modern navigation tools – if you want to have a reasonable chance of surviving the treacherous waters and reaching your destination alive.

In today's challenging business environment, leading a business is the same. Business leaders need a business plan framework that is strong and "seaworthy" – strong enough for surviving the disruptive forces that they face. And it is essential to use planning methodologies that allow for mid-course corrections to keep the business "ship" on track and moving in the right direction in a changing world. Our dynamic business planning process provides these elements.

THE BOOK

This book is divided into five chapters and a conclusion. Each chapter includes several recommended readings offering different perspectives on business planning and references to additional relevant resources.

Chapter 1 is a brief overview that introduces our dynamic planning process, and warns planners about typical business planning pitfalls.

Chapters 2 through 4 are the heart of the book. These chapters describe our planning approach – a step-by-step process that includes appropriate planning methodologies and tools.

Chapter 5 addresses creating a written plan document (Step 6 in our planning process). Although the preparation of the document itself is not our primary focus, some thoughts about it are necessary. Therefore this chapter gives general guidance, shows typical business plan outlines, and provides references to additional resources.

The Conclusion focuses on the "living" business plan – the final step in our dynamic business planning process. It provides suggestions for reviews and mid-course corrections to the plan to keep it relevant and dynamic.

In this book, since it addresses basics, there are similarities to traditional business plan teachings. However as we have emphasized, we focus on the planning process, not the plan. In addition, in selected areas we illustrate specific tools that we have found particularly useful. These focus on topics such as:

- Detailed analysis of industry/market changes, including external forces

- Clearly defined and understood strategic direction and business objectives

- Change management for the evolution of the plan

In addition, this book focuses on a basic business planning process. The framework provided is appropriate for successful navigation in a dynamic business environment, and it is the foundation for combating major crises such as economic downturns. But what we provide is only a starting point. It is intended to provide a "step-in-the-right-direction" for beginning planners and to address issues that more experienced planners may have wrestled with by suggesting thought-provoking actions.

CHAPTER 1

BUSINESS PLANNING OVERVIEW

Chapter 1 is a brief overview that addresses some business planning basics, including a summary of the business planning steps in our process and descriptions of some of the most common planning pitfalls. We start by clarifying what we mean by "Business Plan".

THE BUSINESS PLAN

What is a business plan? This question can be answered in several ways.

A business plan is a document that can be viewed as your **roadmap to success**. It establishes a realistic baseline of where your company is today, identifies end-goals, and describes how to modify the present plan or course of action to reach those goals. In other words, it is a detailed map showing the road you have decided to take to the future. How much detail is needed depends on the destination you have chosen and the terrain.

A business plan also is a tool for optimizing growth and developing businesses according to specific plans and priorities. It can help leaders significantly improve performance, survive crises of various kinds, and even re-invent their businesses if necessary. From this perspective, a business plan can be viewed as a way to control your own destiny.

Bottom line, a business plan is an organized, logical way to look at all of the important aspects of a business. Although its organization and content may vary, a good business plan answers five basic questions:

1. Who are you and where are you now in the real world of business? The answers are derived from realistic status assessments and provide your business baseline.
2. Where do you want to arrive, and when do you expect to get there? The answers are your financial goals and business objectives.
3. How are you going to get from where you are to where you want to be? The answers are the strategies, the programs and the implementation and operational plans – the detailed paths you intend to follow to your goals.
4. What is your current financial picture and what will it be – if you follow your plan? In a literal sense, the answers are the "bottom line."
5. How will you execute your plan? This typically means what are the sources and uses of funds and other resources?

BUSINESS PLAN VALUES/USES

Having a good business plan that is properly documented is vital for any business leader in today's dynamic world. To appreciate the value of a good business plan, one only needs to consider some of its common uses.

We describe the values/uses of a business plan from

two perspectives: first as a sales tool and then as a management tool.

A Business Plan as a Sales Tool

Figure 1: A Business Plan as a Sales Tool

Figure 1 summarizes some of the common uses of a business plan as a sales tool. These uses are described in more detail below.

A business plan is required to obtain financing from external investors. In the case of a start-up company, these investors can range from commercial banks to venture capitalists to the government. However, it's not only start-up companies that need financing. Often business units within large corporations are vying for limited resources. In these cases, a good business plan is essential to obtain needed corporate support.

A business plan can help leaders gain support for start-up ventures or justify new courses of action for existing businesses. It is a well-accepted vehicle to communicate to the outside world the desired actions. For existing businesses, this is particularly important when the new direction is radically different from the old one – a situation that often arises when a strong new competitor appears on the scene or when some other external force (e.g., recession) impacts the business.

A business plan also can be a tool to convince the external world of the value of a business. This is useful for establishing alliances, attracting personnel, and for finding buyers for a business. For these purposes, the audience must believe that the business can do what the plan says.

A Business Plan as a Management Tool

A Business Plan as a
Management Tool for

Setting direction, making
decisions, tracking progress

Prioritizing programs &
allocating resources

Establishing a baseline for
business assessments

Evaluating new growth
opportunities

Communication

Figure 2: A Business Plan as a Management Tool

Figure 2 summarizes some of the common uses of a business plan as a management tool. These uses are described in more detail below.

A business plan establishes goals and sets the direction for a business. It provides a framework for making decisions, defining and prioritizing programs, and allocating resources. It establishes a baseline that allows leaders to track business progress, assess how well goals are being met, and make needed mid-course corrections.

Large companies use business plans to evaluate new growth opportunities and to understand the implications of possible mergers, acquisitions, and divestitures on their core businesses. And for any company or business unit, the planning process can be used to develop ideas about how business should be conducted and to test out different strategies "on paper" before taking costly actions. A business plan also is a communication tool. It is a way to present to the organization (as well as to the outside world) concrete goals and clear strategic direction. It provides the framework for consistency throughout the organization. And, if it is compelling, it produces consensus and a sense of urgency.

KEY BUSINESS PLAN ELEMENTS

Although a business plan can have many purposes and its parts and format can vary, there are three important elements to any good plan:

- **Goals**. These consist of financial targets and key business objectives.
- **Strategies**. These are the approaches to reach the Goals.
- **Programs and Plans**. These are the specific actions to be taken (including tactics) to implement the Strategies.

The rest of the written plan basically is a summary of the information used to create these three elements. The document itself presents all of this information in whatever is the most appropriate way to communicate the plan clearly to the intended audience and to gain their support.

BUSINESS PLANNING STEPS

How do you generate the key business plan elements and turn them into a viable and "living" business plan document? This is what our *Dynamic Business Planning Process* does. This process consists of seven steps, as shown in **Figure 3**. These steps are independent of the organization and of the specific contents of the final business plan.

Figure 3: Dynamic Business Planning Steps

If your business is a new venture, you may be starting from the very beginning with each step of the process. But even if your business is established and you already have a complete plan, it is important to keep in mind that business planning is an iterative process.

The world is changing and so must you. To keep your plan viable and to keep the target in your sights, you need to periodically re-visit each step of the process. Therefore, let's look at each of these steps in a little more detail.

Step 1: The Baseline.

Establishing a realistic picture of your current and near-future business is the first step in the dynamic planning process and is the subject of Chapter 2. This step involves taking a critical look at your business and industry and then making a realistic assessment of the health of your business and the status of business world surrounding it – the Industry, the market segments, key players and competitors.

It is particularly important to understand external forces that are or could be impacting your business – things like the economy, government regulations, and technology advancements. In addition, this realistic picture includes projections of your business direction and performance based on your current business plan.

In other words, this snapshot of your business world is your "Baseline" and serves as your STARTING POINT.

Step 2: The Goals.

The second step in our dynamic planning process is all about establishing clear financial goals and business objectives. This involves determining the desired future "arrival point" for your business and realistic timelines for getting there.

The process for doing this includes exploring alternative goals (or future business arrival points) and choosing the best. For example, one goal may represent a larger future business (growth) while another may represent a smaller but more profitable business, and yet another may represent a business in a totally different market segment, and so on.

The challenge with goal-setting is choosing the best from alternatives like these. Making this decision is not always simple. One must consider factors such as stockholder requirements, availability of resources, and timing desired for reaching the goal. In other words, for each alternative one must consider not only the desired arrival point, but also the realism of the stretch required. This step in our planning process is covered in the first section of Chapter 3.

At the conclusion of this step, the goals are defined. In other words you have determined the direction you will take to lead your business into the future.

Step 3: The Gap.

After completing Steps 1 and 2, you will have determined your business baseline and established your business goals. The distance between your current business performance and your goals is what we call the "Gap". In other words, the gap is your current business plan shortfall.

Specifically, if your business is an established one, from your business assessment in Step 1 you will have a realistic projection of your future business performance – your expected arrival point assuming that you continue to follow your current plan. If you compare that to your desired arrival point, you have the gap. Identifying this shortfall allows you to answer the question: Is your business well positioned for the future with your current course of action or do you need to change your business plan? If you are just starting your business, the goals themselves define the gap.

At this point, understanding the nature of the gap is just as important as understanding its magnitude. Questions to consider include: What issues are preventing you from reaching your goals? What new challenges will your new direction create? Will your new course change the competitive environment? By considering your real starting point, along with the answers to these questions, you should be able to determine whether your chosen goal is attainable or it should be re-considered. Keep in mind that the bigger the gap, the bigger the challenge! You also need to be sure that the rewards justify the risk. The process for determining and understanding your business gap is covered in the second section of Chapter 3.

Step 4: Bridging the Gap.

Once your business gap is identified and understood, the next step is to determine what strategy to use to change your business course to "Bridge the Gap".

What do we mean by "Strategy"? A strategy can be defined as a "fundamental" and long-term plan designed to achieve a particular goal. For a start-up business, developing an innovative strategy is a key piece of a compelling business plan. If your business is an established one you already have a strategy that you are pursuing, whether it is explicit or implicit. However, if you have determined from Step 3 that you also have a significant gap, the question in front of you is not whether you should change your strategy, but HOW you should change it.

There is never just one simple choice. There usually are many different possible strategies that can be pursued in an attempt to attain a company's end goal. Possibilities range from just optimizing your internal operations to changing your entire business focus.

In determining which strategy is best, the type of information collected in Step 1 (The Baseline) is essential. Many factors must be considered, including competitive reactions, resource requirements, timing, and risk. The third segment of Chapter 3 provides guidelines for this step of the dynamic business planning process.

Step 5: Action Plans.

The next step in our dynamic planning process is to develop action plans based on the chosen goals, objectives, and strategies.

What are "Action Plans"? They are the short-term priorities and detailed plans for specific programs that will implement the strategies. In other words, they are the heart of a good business plan.

Action plans must be detailed, self-consistent, and doable. The programs must be well defined, the priorities must be clear, specific responsibilities must be assigned, and appropriate resources must be available when needed.

And last but not least, all parts of the business must be operating on the same page – the same goals, the same strategies supporting these goals, the same program plans and priorities for implementing the strategies. In other words the plans and priorities for each business function (marketing, manufacturing, R&D, etc.) must be integrated, coordinated, and consistent with the overall business framework. These are key success factors for good action plans.

Creating integrated action plans and verifying the expected outcomes from them are the subjects of Chapter 4. In essence, action plans are your detailed roadmap to your future business success.

Step 6: The Business Plan Document.

Step 6 of our planning process focuses on creating a useful business plan document. In essence, this step is the sum of all the previous steps: a realistic business baseline, clear goals, well thought out strategies, and detailed action plans. These are the pieces needed for the "Business Plan

Document".

Which of these pieces you emphasize, how you sum them together, how you format the document, how you write the text – it's up to you. It is your challenge to create a compelling and convincing business guide that is appropriate for your unique set of circumstances. Guidelines for doing this are given in Chapter 5.

Step 7: The "Living" Business Plan.

Now you have a written plan. The final challenge is to execute your plan. Or is it? Step 7 of our process addresses creating a "living" business plan. This includes methodologies for monitoring results and modifying your plan as appropriate to keep you on track to you goals.

In today's dynamic world, your plan also needs to be dynamic – what we call a living business plan. In other words, your business plan must be adaptable as your business situation changes. You must have methodologies to determine the need for and to make mid-course corrections.

Therefore, the last step of dynamic business planning is to develop and embrace a cyclic planning process: execute » monitor » revise » repeat. This cycle creates your living business plan - the subject of Chapter 6. It is this cycle that makes the business planning process a dynamic one.

BUSINESS PLANNING PITFALLS

Some words of caution: Before delving into the details of our dynamic planning process, you need to BE AWARE OF PLANNING PITFALLS! The remainder of this section describes four of the most common causes for the failure of "conventional" business or strategic plans. Because these mistakes can be deadly, it is important to keep them in mind as you move forward with the planning process.

Pitfall 1: Lack of Realism.

The most common failure of business plans is the "lack of realism" in the plan. Most plans are over-optimistic. They don't take into account the changing business environment, they don't anticipate counter-moves by competitors, and they don't adequately account for program risk (actual performance, cost, and/or timing). This results in what is commonly called the "hockey stick" forecast – projected sales/profits increasing slowly in the short term with large and rapid increases at some time in the future.

Such forecasts look great on paper and may serve to gain needed business support in the short term. However, lack of promised results when the future becomes "today" discourages potential investors and may jeopardize the very existence of a company, especially in disruptive times.

The best way to avoid this trap starts with establishing a realistic baseline (Chapter 2), and continues with the development of detailed and verified action plans (Chapter 4).

Pitfall 2: Lack of Consistency.

Another common failure in business plans is the lack of overall consistency. In other words, the pieces of the business plan "puzzle" do not fit together in the framework of the overall plan. What exactly do we mean?

Often program plans and timelines don't adequately take into account available resources and capabilities. Or, just as common, different parts of the organization have conflicting priorities and goals. Issues such as these often result from the lack of alignment and coordination among the Functions of the company. For example, in spite of a business plan that calls for focus on low cost products, there may be a marketing plan promoting the sale of premium products, which the manufacturing equipment cannot produce.

How can this type of pitfall be avoided? The answer lies with clearly understood Goals and Strategies (Chapter 3) and Integrated Action Plans (Chapter 4).

Pitfall 3: Words Instead of Actions.

Often companies take a considerable amount of time in writing extensive business plans that focus on elaborate Goals, grandly-worded Strategies, and financial projections showing amazing business success.

However, achieving this business success often is based on fuzzy actions. In other words, the IMPLEMENTATION specifics are not defined. Programs have not been thoroughly planned, priorities and responsibilities are unclear, and coordinated cross-functional efforts have not been established. This makes the "planned" success highly unlikely.

The solution: specific Action Plans (addressed in Chapter 4).

Pitfall 4: Lack of Mid-Course Corrections.

The business environment changes constantly. New competitors are born, other competitors go out of business, customer requirements evolve, technology advances, and so on. To address these continual changes, even without the occurrence of a sudden disruptive event, a business plan must evolve with time. A rigid plan is doomed to obsolescence within a few months of its inception – a dead document lost in someone's filing cabinet.

To say it another way, no business plan is good forever. Aiming toward a target (goal) with a fixed plan is like trying to drive a car without steering. At best you are likely to end up at an unexpected destination. At worst you will drive off a cliff.

The solution: a "living" business plan created by a cyclic process (addressed in the Conclusion).

SUMMARY

A business plan is a formal statement of a set of business goals, the reasons why it is believed that they are attainable, and the plan for reaching those goals. This plan can be focused on the external world or the internal one, it can be both strategic and operational, and it can have multiple purposes and multiple audiences.

Bottom line, a good business plan is your customized "Roadmap to Success" with whatever format and focus meets the unique needs of your business. The remaining chapters of this book lead you through the steps of our dynamic planning process – the end result of which will be your "Living Business Plan".

CHAPTER 2

YOUR BUSINESS BASELINE
(Step 1)

Establishing your business Baseline is **STEP 1** in our dynamic business planning process and is the subject of Chapter 2. **Figure 4** illustrates the key elements included in your business world that make up your baseline.

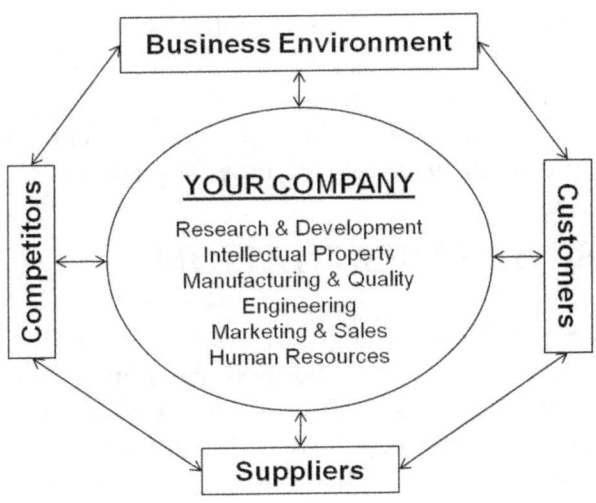

Figure 4: Your Business World

First there is your internal environment: your company – its makeup and its business. Then there is the external business world in which your company exists. This consists of customers, competitors, suppliers, and the business environment (other external forces impacting your company such as technology, regulations, and the economy).

As the figure shows, all of these elements are interconnected. They influence each other and impact your business. This is your business world and understanding it is what this step in our dynamic planning process is all about.

To help you create this understanding, Chapter 2 is divided into four sections: Business Description, Financial Performance, Internal Assessment, and Industry & Markets. At the end of the chapter you will have answered questions about your business such as:

- Who are you? What business are you in and how do you carry out your business?
- Where are you now? What are your capabilities and financial results?
- Where is your current path leading? How well positioned are you for the future?

When you have realistic answers to these questions you will have established "Your Business Baseline." This is the first building block for your business plan.

BUSINESS DESCRIPTION

The first topic to investigate in your quest for a realistic business baseline is your business description. You may think that a description of your business is obvious, but is it? Can you clearly and concisely define what business you are in and how you do business? Has this framework for your business been intentional or has your business just evolved when the opportunities presented themselves?

To determine whether or not you would benefit by changing your business framework and/or strategies (addressed in Chapter 3), you first need to have a clear understanding of your current business definition and your business model – the key elements of your business description.

Business Definition.

Who or what are you? This is the most basic question about your business. The answer is your business definition. It defines both constraints and opportunities for business development. More specifically, a good business definition answers questions such as:

- What Business are you in?
  - o Who are your customers?
  - o What need do you address?
  - o How do you meet that need?
- What products do you provide to what markets?
- What is the scope of your business?
  - o Industries
  - o Market segments
  - o Geography

Looking at it from a different perspective, a business definition can be conceptual or based on technologies, products, customers or markets. A conceptual business definition describes what your business hopes to become and how. A technology based business definition stresses your technology core competencies. A product based business definition focuses on the products or services you offer while a customer based business definition focuses on the kinds of people or businesses you serve and the needs they have. A market based business definition defines your business in terms of your current market segments, including geographic distribution.

Your business definition does not need to be lengthy, but it should be clear. It can be very simple: My Company provides Product X to Market Y. However some detail is more useful: My Company is a high quality, contract manufacturer of electronic devices for the health care industry. Or, My Company designs and sells innovative products to help generate a healthy indoor climate for commercial office buildings.

Bottom line, you should be able to write your company's (or business') current business definition in no more than TWO sentences. The following reference provides a more detailed look at the concept of "Business Definition":

> *www.12manage.com/methods_abell_three_dimensional_busi ness_definition.html* (1)

Business Model

Now let's turn to your "Business Model". How do you bring products to life and how do you profit from them? This description of the way you conduct business is your business model and is the baseline for your business planning on the operational side.

Just like the business definition, the business model defines both constraints and opportunities for business development. Let's look at the elements of a business model in a little more detail.

Your business model answers the broad question: How do you do business? More specifically it answers questions such as:

- How do you "obtain" the products you sell? Do you outsource R&D and/or manufacturing, do you sell products obtained from someone else, or do you do everything yourself?

- How do you reach your customers? Do you have your own sales force, sell through distribution, or do business over the Internet?
- Do you rely on any special alliances or relationships with customers, "middlemen" or decision makers?
- How do you make money? What are the revenue streams and what is your cost structure?

An equally important part of your business model is your framework for creating value – your value proposition. In other words, what benefits do you offer to your customers – performance, price, response time, or?

Here again, concise and clear is better that a long document. You should be able to describe your current business model in ONE paragraph. For a more detailed description of the concept of business model, along with examples, see:

en.wikipedia.org/ wiki/ Business_model (2)

FINANCIAL PERFORMANCE

The second part of the baseline is the financial performance of your business – the past, the present, and your projections of future performance based on your current business plan. This section highlights the kinds of numbers you should look at and the kinds of questions you should address, but teaching detailed financial analysis is beyond the scope of this guide. We suggest you include a financial expert in the process for creating a realistic financial picture of your business.

What financial information should you use to assess your business' performance? Some of the standard measures used by businesses include: Sales and Profits, Cash Flow, Break-Even Analysis, ROCE, ROE, EVA, and

Earnings per Share. But your business probably already has defined financial goals. We suggest that you pick financial measures that reflect those goals and are appropriate for your specific business situation.

Using your chosen measures, first look at past and current performance versus your forecast. Then look at the 5-year forecast, including the assumptions that are part of that forecast. We'll come back to this forecast in Chapter 3, but for now you should be assessing the likelihood of achieving that forecast.

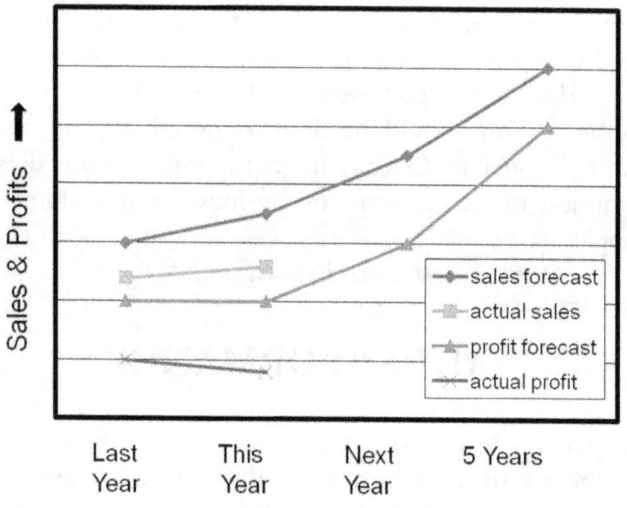

Figure 5: Financial Performance – an Example

A graphic example of one kind of simple financial analysis is shown in **Figure 5**.This figure shows sales and profits of a company over time, compared with its forecasts. Graphs like this are good way to illustrate financial performance using your chosen financial indicators.

For this hypothetical case, there are some obvious questions that the past and current performances raise. These include:

- Are the current forecasts realistic?
- What specifically will cause sales/profits to increase?
- What assumptions were used to create the forecast?
- What are the key success factors for keeping on target and meeting forecast?
- What are the critical issues?

These are the kinds of checking questions you should be asking related to your own business financial performance. You may not have the answers to all of these questions yet, but after completing the next section (Internal Assessment), you should have more of that baseline information.

INTERNAL ASSESSMENT

This section focuses on guidance for evaluating functional capabilities (operations), assessing products (existing and future), and determining intellectual property strengths. This internal assessment, coupled with the financial analysis, is what we call a "business audit".

Functional Evaluation

A company's operations are made up of a number of functions such as Research and Development (R&D), Engineering, Manufacturing, Quality, Marketing, Sales, Human Resources, Finance, etc. How many different functions exist and which ones they are vary from company to company or business to business.

Whatever the structure, often a company is unbalanced. For example it may have most of its capabilities and strengths in R&D or in Marketing and Sales – at the expense of the other functions. The right balance among the various functions of a company, relative to what the company objectives are, is an important factor for business success. An un-biased examination of the company's internal strengths and weaknesses is the starting point in assessing this balance. This knowledge can then be used for business re-direction that leverages the company's core competencies.

Examples of topics that often need specific attention are R&D core competencies, Manufacturing processes and productivity, human resource skill sets, and Marketing and Sales effectiveness. In addition, resource allocation and adequacy of functional plans are often issues. But each business is unique. Therefore it is up to you to determine the functions and areas that are most important for your business and what process you will use for evaluation. However, we strongly recommend that you include outside and un-biased "auditors" in your assessments.

The outcome of your functional assessments should include a clear understanding of your operational strengths, weaknesses, and critical issues.

Product Assessment

Now that you have a realistic picture of your operational capabilities, it's time to take a critical look at your products – both individually and collectively, both existing products and future ones.

The key factors that usually need to be evaluated for existing products include: performance versus competition, adequacy of the technology employed, proprietary position, quality, and maturity. For future products (those in development or being planned), these same factors are important, but there are additional factors to consider such as expected returns, timing, and risk involved (probability of success). However, depending on your particular products (existing or future), the list will vary. Again, it's up to you to decide what factors are most important for a focused assessment of your products.

In addition to assessing your individual products, it's important to take a look at your product portfolio. There are many different ways to carry out this kind of assessment. However we find that a "visual" comparison often is most useful. As an example, **Figure 6** shows one way to look at your product portfolio strength by assessing product performance and maturity at the same time.

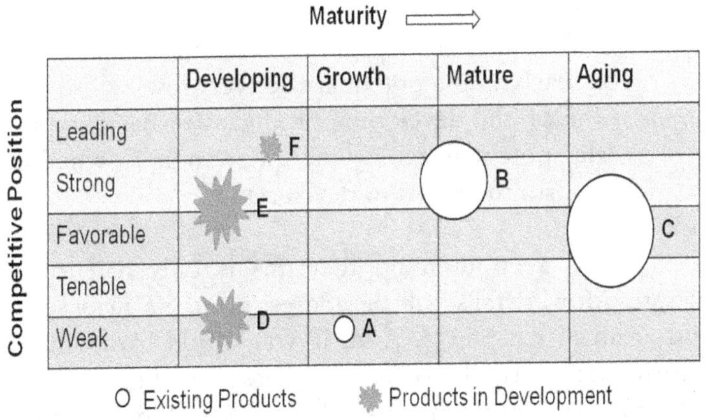

Figure 6: Assessing Your Product Portfolio

The competitive position (vertical axis) of each product (from "leading" through "weak") is plotted versus the degree of maturity (horizontal axis) of that product (from "developing" through "aging"). The sizes of the circles and starbursts represent the actual sales of existing products and the potential sales at maturity of products in development.

The competitive position of existing products (the circles) in this example refers to performance of your products versus existing competitive products. The competitive position of products in development (starbursts) is an educated guess based on projections about what competition will be when your new products are commercialized.

Maturity (horizontal axis) refers to sales dynamics: growing, stable (mature), decreasing (aging), or potential (developing).

Three issues are highlighted in this example:

1. None of the developing products have the potential to replace the sales of the mature/aging products (not a good growth outlook for the business).
2. One of the developing products (D) will have a very weak competitive position, making the probability of reaching the potential sales very low.
3. One of the developing products (F) has very small sales potential, raising the question as to whether it is worth the effort to develop it.

And keep in mind that this is only half of the picture. More details will be addressed in the next section and again in Chapter 3. And, if you would like additional information related to product assessments, the book *"Winning at New Products"* by R.G. Cooper, *Perseus Publishing 2001*, is an excellent reference (3).

Intellectual Property

Before your internal assessment is complete, it is important to evaluate your company's intellectual property. This is even more important today than in the past. Why is that?

As technology advances on many fronts, more and more businesses are turning into increasingly "high-tech" operations. In addition, the pace of business is faster. Although no kind of intellectual property will protect its holder from competition forever, in a business environment where speed is a key success factor, patents can be effective weapons for *slowing down* the competition. Therefore, in this new kind of environment, intellectual property has increased importance as a strategic weapon. And intellectual property means more than just patents. It includes things such as trademarks and brands, copyrights, and even business practices. These different kinds of intellectual property can be used to nurture and protect your business and to block others from entry. But, keep in mind, intellectual property of others can provide a barrier to your business development. It is essential in today's dynamic environment that intellectual property considerations be factored into not only product-related decisions but also total business decisions.

Typical questions to ask for existing products include: Is there any intellectual property protection and if so, how strong is it? How can this protection be used to provide additional benefit?

For new products being developed these same questions apply, but equally important questions are: Do others have intellectual property that will limit or block the new product? How can intellectual property be developed or strengthened for the new product?

This completes the Internal Assessment part of creating your business baseline. At this point, by using the guidance presented in this section you should have a detailed picture of your internal capabilities, strengths, and weaknesses. Therefore you should be able to list your organization's core competencies (key capabilities), to summarize the key strengths and weaknesses of your product portfolio, and to identify the internal issues that are having the greatest negative impact on you business.

If you would like some additional insight into internal assessment, we suggest the article *"How to Appraise Your Organization Capabilities and Disabilities"* by C. Christensen, *Harvard Business Review, June 11, 1997* (4). This article provides an excellent and somewhat different perspective on Internal Assessment.

EXTERNAL ASSESSMENT

You have now completed three of the four legs of establishing your Business Baseline: Business Description, Financial Performance, and Internal Assessment. In this last leg, you will explore your external business world.

In the first section we address creating (or reviewing) the big picture – an Industry/Market analysis. The second section focuses on understanding your Competitors. And finally, the third section brings it together with a look at Your Competitive Position.

Industry/Market Analysis

Many excellent books have been written on methodologies for detailed industry and market analysis. In this brief guide, we will not attempt that level of explanation, but instead will provide a "big picture" overview to point you in the right direction.

First of all, there are many factors that need to be considered for the industry and markets that you address. These include:

- Industry Definition and Scope
- Market Segments
- Key Players/Participants
- Geographic Differences
- Impact of external forces
- Industry/Market Trends
- Market Size and Growth
- Market Needs
- Key Success Factors

There are many sources of this kind of information that you need. Internet searching can help you locate most of them. With this information you should be able to answer questions like: How big is the market and is it growing? How crowded is the playing field? Are there "external forces" (technology, economy, regulatory, etc.) that are changing or likely to change the business environment? Collecting this kind of information in detail and developing an in-depth understanding of your business arena is time well-spent.

And, even if you already have a business plan for which you once performed this analysis, it's important to revisit the situation. Many companies fail because they do not CONTINUOUSLY monitor their surroundings. The market situation yesterday may be very different from the situation today or tomorrow.

The following suggestions can help you get started and/or give you a different perspective on industry and market analysis. First, we suggest that you read a summary of *"Porter's 5 Forces Model for Industry Analysis"*. This is a good summary of Michael Porter's well-known model for analyzing industries. You can find this article at: *www.quickmba.com/strategy/porter.shtml* (5). After reading this, you should be able to list the key barriers to entry for your industry/market, identify potential substitutes for your products, and describe supplier power in your business arena.

In addition, we recommend Michael Porter's book *"Competitive Strategy, Techniques for Analyzing Industries and Competitors"* by Michael Porter, The Free Press (Simon & Schuster), *1980* (6). This is THE classic text on industry/market analysis and is an excellent reference book.

Competitor Profiles

Next, your competition. Understanding your competition – their strengths, their weaknesses, their business strategies, and their new products under development – is key to your business success. The type of information you should have about each key player includes: market share, product offerings (types, performance, and pricing), resources, technology strength, business strategies (including pricing), and overall strengths and weaknesses.

Questions you should be able to answer include: How many direct competitors do you have and who are they? Are there geographic differences? What are your competitors' investment and pricing strategies? What are their presumed cost structures? How do they balance risk versus reward? Are they developing "Disruptive Technologies"? And equally important, what about potential competitors and indirect competition? Who is likely to be your biggest threat in the future?

Again, Michael Porter's book (reference 6) is an excellent reference for competitive analysis. However, finding information on your competitors is another challenge. The Internet can help. Here is a reference for a good summary on competitive analysis and sources of information:

www.sba.gov/smallbusinessplanner/manage/marketandprice
/SERV_COMPANAYLSIS.html (7)

Your Competitive Position

Now that you have collected the basic information on your competitors, it's time to take a realistic look at your competitive position. In this section we illustrate two of the many different ways to compare your business to that of your direct competitors. However DO NOT forget to consider your indirect and future competitors. We'll come back to those in Chapter 3 when we look at developing strategies.

So first, consider market share. Market share is often used as a key indicator of competitive position. **Figure 7** shows a hypothetical example of how this information might be displayed and used. It illustrates the current situation for you and your 3 key competitors and projects the status at some point in the future – often 5 years. The sizes of the circles represent the relative sizes of the market at the two different time points.

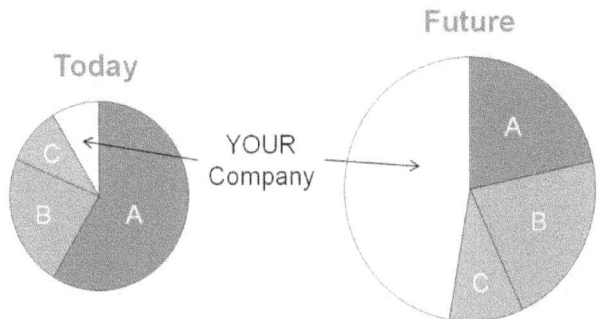

Figure 7: Market Share – Yours and Theirs

This figure shows two important things: The overall market is growing, making it potentially attractive (both for you and your competitors), and your share increases dramatically, primarily at the expense of Company A. It raises the question about how realistic this picture is. Do you have data to support the projected market growth? What specifically will cause Company A to lose ground while you gain it? These are questions you need to consider.

Your competitive strength is another way to look at competitive position, as we illustrate in **Figure 8** on the next page. Again your company is compared to your three key competitors. However this time, instead of market share, three other factors are considered – the products offered, the kind and quality of services provided, and the technology basis for the products. Where do these factors come from? They are what you have determined to be the key success factors for the market you address.

In each category, you rank your Company and the competition (specifying who is #1 and so on). Then, the numbers for each company are added. The **lowest** total score indicates the strongest Company overall. Note: If one of the factors is much more important than the others, the numbers can be weighted as appropriate.

	Company A	Company B	Company C	Your Company
Product Offerings	1	2	3	4
Service	1	4	2	3
Technology	2	3	4	1
TOTAL	4	9	9	8

Figure 8: Your Competitive Strength

This example shows two important things: Company A is the clear leader, while your company is back with the rest of the pack. And, Your Company is the technology leader, but last with the products you offer. Now, if you refer back to the market share information, you can see that product offerings might be more important than you thought – at least it's something to keep in mind as you proceed with the planning process.

These kinds of analyses or others should enable you to identify and understand your company's key strengths and weaknesses compared to your main competitors.

At this point you should clearly understand the process to create your realistic business baseline – Step 1 in our dynamic business planning process. Although the suggestions and examples by themselves are not enough to establish this baseline, expanding on them will allow you to determine a realistic Starting Point for your Business Plan.

The next step: Where do you want to arrive?

CHAPTER 3

GOALS, GAPS, STRATEGIES

This Chapter describes the next three steps in our dynamic business planning process:

- **Step 2**: Goal-Setting
- **Step 3**: Determining The Gap
- **Step 4**: Developing Strategies

To actually carry out these process steps, you need all of the information used in determining your business baseline. Without this foundation it is difficult, if not impossible, to formulate goals that are achievable but ambitious and to develop strategies that have a good probability of allowing you to reach those goals.

So, let's assume that you have that business baseline. In other words, you know your starting point. Then the question becomes: "Where do you want to arrive?" Answering this question is Step 2 in our planning process.

STEP 2: GOAL-SETTING

After determining a REALISTIC business baseline (starting

point), establishing clear and realistic goals (the chosen arrival point) is the next step in our dynamic business planning process. This step involves exploring alternative goals and picking the best.

Why is goal-setting the second step in our process instead of the first? For each alternative arrival point (goal), you must consider the realism of the stretch required to achieve that goal. To be able to judge this, you must have a clear understanding of where your business is today. In other words, before making your final choice of goals, you must assess whether or not those goals are indeed attainable.

Now, what is a goal? A goal is a clear target or objective, and achieving that goal is considered success. However, for it to be achievable, a goal must make sense (be reasonable) and it must be specific, measurable, and have a defined time frame. Business goals are generally either financial goals or business objectives. These are explored in more detail in the next two sections.

Financial Goals

The primary goals of most businesses are financial ones. These can be measured in a number of different ways. Some of the most typical categories are those that we outlined in the Financial Performance section of Chapter 2: Sales and Profits, Cash Flow, Break-Even Analysis, ROCE, ROE, EVA, and Earnings per Share.

One of the most common types of financial goals is sales and/or profits. Here are a few examples of how such goals might be formulated to meet the criteria of specific, measurable, and with a defined time frame:

- 15% profit within 5 years
- Profit growth ($$) of 40% in 4 years
- Sales growth ($$) of 50% in 3 years

- Breakeven in 2 years

Although sales and profit goals are common, they are not always the most appropriate ones. It is important to keep in mind that different types of businesses measure financial success in different ways. For example, grocery stores often target return on assets.

Whatever the measure, it is usually best to have no more than three financial goals. But what is right for your business depends on your specific situation. Just keep in mind: These are the goals the business plan must strive to achieve. These goals must be clearly defined, be consistent with each other, and be achievable for your specific business situation. Assessing this will be revisited in Chapter 4.

Business Objectives

We call goals that are not directly financial ones, Business Objectives. These kinds of goals are sometimes considered secondary since they often represent the beginnings of the strategies to achieve the financial goals. However they are important to consider in this stage of the planning process since they can pose business constraints as well as opportunities.

Some typical business objectives fall into categories such as growth, market share, new products, technology, and "green". Here are some examples of specific and measurable business objectives with defined timeframes:

- Sales growth (units) of 50% in 2 years
- Market share leader (measured by $$ sales) within 4 years
- 35% of sales from new products within 5 years
- 50% of sales ($$) outside the US within 3 years
- 40% of sales ($$) from e-business by the end of the year

- 2 new stores open and profitable within 2 years
- All food products certified organic within 4 years.

These are just a few of the possibilities. Your goal-setting challenge is choosing a very limited number of the best and most important financial goals and business objectives for your business from among the many alternatives.

If good goals have already been set for your business – great! If not, **now is the time to do it**. It is impossible to plan your business trip if you have no idea where you want to go. Just remember, good goals are specific and measurable. They have a defined endpoint. And, although goals may be challenging, they must be attainable.

Are your proposed goals attainable? It depends on the "Gap". Determining that gap is Step 3 in our dynamic business planning process.

STEP 3: DETERMINING THE GAP

If you have been following our planning process, you now have established both your starting point (Your Business Baseline) and your chosen arrival point (Goals). In this step of our process we address determining both the magnitude and the nature of the "Gap". What is this gap? It is the distance and terrain between where your business is and where you want it to be. How do you determine this gap for your business situation?

For start-up businesses, determining the gap is simple. The starting point is zero, so the gap is the entire distance from where the business is today to the goals. In other words, the goals define the gap. However, for established businesses, the situation is somewhat more complex. For ongoing businesses, the gap is the difference between the realistic projected "endpoint" of the current business plan and the goals. In other words, the gap is the shortfall of the current business plan.

So what is the size and nature of your business gap, and what are the causes?

The Gap: Its Size and Nature

As stated above, for start-up businesses, the goals define the size of the gap and its nature. If this is your business situation, you can focus on the causes of your gap.

As also stated above, for established businesses, the gap is the current business plan shortfall. To determine what this shortfall is, a **realistic** forecast based on actual baseline business performance is essential. In other words, you need to be able to project what the most probable performance of your business will be at specific points in the future – *if the current course of action is unchanged.*

Then, the difference between your projected results and the goals defines the size and nature of your business gap. Once you know this, you can start to assess whether or not your goals are attainable or should be re-considered. Remember, the bigger the gap, the bigger the challenge.

The Gap: Its Causes

But the size of the gap is only one factor to be considered. Equally important are the causes of the gap. Identifying and understanding these causes will help determine how drastic the corrective actions need to be in order to achieve the goals and whether or not the goals need modification.

For example, common causes for gaps are *internal operational issues*. These often can be corrected with appropriate changes, requiring only minor modification to the business plan. Examples of these kinds of issues include resources not aligned with priorities, operational efficiency, new product timeliness, manufacturing cost/waste, pricing.

Business constraints are another common cause for gaps. These usually are more difficult to deal with than operational issues. Often business constraints such as an unchangeable business definition, CEO's rules, stockholder expectations, or limited risk tolerance require a totally new business plan to close the gap. That may not be possible. Then, the goals need to be revised and the gap re-examined.

Last on our list of common causes of gaps are **external forces**. Because this is often a major cause of problems, it is dealt with here in more detail.

It's important to remember that a business is not operating in isolation. There are a number of external forces that help or hinder its course and often are the primary causes of the business plan shortfall (the Gap).

Figure 9 lists some EVOLUTIONARY changes that can become very important external forces, a little at the time, without a company realizing it until it is too late for an adequate response. Also listed are examples of DISRUPTIVE forces – those which can suddenly and significantly alter the business environment.

External Forces

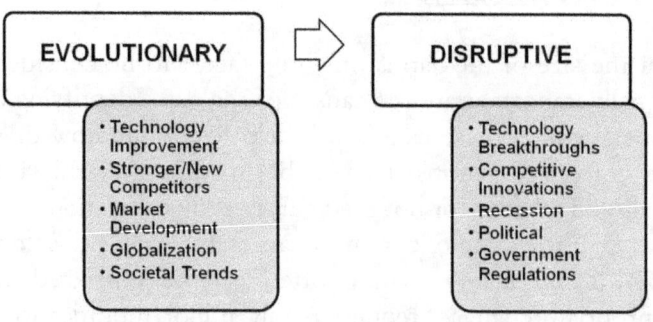

Figure 9: External Forces – Some Examples

Although External Forces will be an important consideration in the next step of our process (Determining Strategies), it also is important to consider them when doing a gap analysis. There are two key questions that need to be answered:

1. Are there external forces (evolutionary or disruptive) that are causing all or part of your business plan shortfall?
2. Are there external forces developing that might negatively impact your business performance in the time before you reach your goals?

After answering these questions, there is one final question: Do you still think your goals are realistic and attainable? If the gap is big enough or if the actions to close it are drastic, perhaps the goals are unrealistic and need to be reconsidered. If so, Step 2 and Step 3 should be repeated. When you are satisfied, you should have clear and specific goals, know the key success factors for achieving those goals, and be able to identify the critical issues related to external forces that your business must consider. At this point you are ready for Step 4: Developing Strategies.

If you would like some additional information on common risks associated with external forces, we suggest the article: "*Countering the Biggest Risk of All*" *by A. Slywotzky and J. Drzik, Harvard Business Review, April 2005* (8).

STEP 4: DEVELOPING STRATEGIES

Once the goals have been established and the gap identified and understood, the next step is to consider alternative strategies for bridging that gap. Keep in mind that once you have determined that you do indeed have a gap, the question is not whether you should change your strategies, but HOW you should change them. In other words, you have recognized that you must change your course in order to achieve your goals. Now the challenge is to decide what direction is the best to take.

Step 4 addresses that challenge by considering three aspects of developing strategies: competitive forces, different types of alternative strategies, and making choices.

Competitive Forces

Figure 10: Competitive Forces Driving the Business Game

In Chapter 1 (Industry/Market Analysis section of External Assessment) we introduced the concept of Porter's 5 Forces model for Industry structural analysis (Reference 5). **Figure 10** illustrates another way to look at this model.

It shows the forces driving competition – the forces that create rivalry in the "game" of business. These competitive forces include: the threat of new entrants, the bargaining power of buyers, the bargaining power of suppliers, the threat of substitute products, and other external forces in your business environment.

This way of looking at your industry/market is not

only a good tool for industry/competitive analysis but also serves as a basis for developing strategies.

Alternative Strategies

Once you understand competitive forces, the challenge is to develop strategies for combating and/or using them to create a competitive advantage that propels your business towards its goals. What are some of the alternative game-changing actions for creating competitive advantage – for changing your business "game" to bridge your gap? They fall into categories such as:

- changing the rules
- changing the players
- changing the added values
- changing the geography
- changing the technology
- expanding your business area

These are all actions that you can consider for changing your business game. To learn more about approaches such as these, we recommend the article "*The Right Game: Use Game Theory to Shape Strategy*" by *A. Brandenburger and B. Nalebuff, Harvard Business Review, July-August 1995* (9). This is NOT a theoretical and mathematical paper. It is an understandable article that starts from a modification of Porter's 5 Forces model and explores the game-changing actions highlighted above.

But what kinds of changes should you consider? What alternative strategies should you investigate as bridges for your particular business gap?

As the article referenced above outlines, there are three general categories of strategies for combating an industry's competitive forces. To summarize, competitive advantage can be created by:

1. **Cost/Value Relationship** (providing lower cost or higher value)
2. **Differentiation** (offering or doing something that is considered unique)
3. **Focus** (narrowing the focus of your business to a particular geography or market segment where your business has a key strength, or broadening the business focus to create a bigger opportunity, or even changing your business focus to create a new kind of opportunity)

Consider first **cost/value** actions, or in other words "changing the added values". This type of strategy could involve outsourcing or selling through distribution or any number of other changes to your business model. Or it could mean optimizing your own internal operations (increased productivity, higher quality) or increasing the performance of existing products (product modification).

Next – **differentiation**. Although "changing the technology" to create new products is the most common strategy here, "changing the rules" through an innovative business model or a disruptive business practice can also be effective (e.g., being the first to sell books on the internet with no physical store). Note: If these kinds of changes are dramatic enough, often they will result in the players also being changed.

Finally, there is **focus** – either more or less or different. Defining your business differently (changing your business definition) and/or establishing alliances of various kinds can either provide for a stronger presence in a more focused segment or can open up larger business opportunities. These actions can change the geography and change the players and their relative positions. Note: broadening your focus usually requires expanding your business definition. We explore this in more detail in the next section.

Expanding Your Business Definition

Since expanding/changing your business definition is a growth strategy of increasing importance in today's fast-paced competitive environment, it is important to clarify what this action involves and how best to approach it.

However, it is important to keep in mind that business definition expansion does not guarantee success. The way you choose to expand your business is key, so there are several important factors to consider before taking action.

The first factor to consider when seeking to expand your business definition is the "**type**" of business. For various reasons (environmental, political, or whatever else) some business areas may be considered unacceptable. The reasons these are "forbidden" don't matter, but they are off limits. Only businesses acceptable to "management" can be considered as expansion areas.

Next, consider the **risk**. To have a reasonable probability of success in a new business area, it should be somewhat associated with your existing business. Trying to achieve your Goals in unfamiliar territory where you cannot rely on your core competencies, leads to frequent failure. In addition, different organizations have different risk tolerances. You must understand yours and judge new business areas accordingly. Businesses judged to present acceptable risk can be considered as expansion areas.

Now the **financials**. Here the intensity of competition and the general financial characteristics of the particular business area (e.g., typical profits, growth, etc.) are important to consider. Only business areas where acceptable financial results are probable should be considered for expansion.

The overlap of the "business areas" identified by combining the above three factors defines the acceptable area for expanding your business definition. **Figure 11** illustrates graphically what we have just described in words.

Starting with all businesses (the largest ellipse), you identify those kinds that are acceptable – a subset of all businesses. Then, considering that subset, you determine which businesses have acceptable financials. Finally you determine those that have acceptable risk. That smaller business world (the area in gray) is the area within which (presumably) your current business falls. And the part of the gray ellipse that is outside of your current business ellipse, defines the acceptable expansion area for your business. The types of businesses that fall within this expansion area are those to consider when seeking to stretch your business definition.

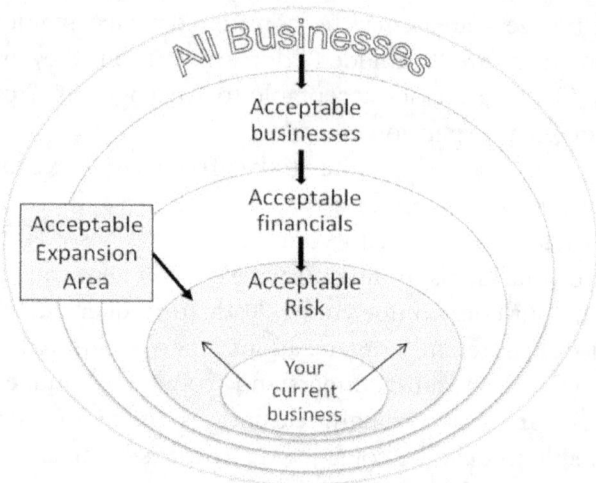

Figure 11: Business Definition Expansion

However, expanding your business definition is just one possible strategy. To conclude this section with a broader view on alternative strategies we have two additional articles to suggest:

- *"Why Companies Should Have Open Business Models"* by H. *Chesbrough, MITSloan Management Review, Winter 2007* (10)
- *"Hardball: Five Killer Strategies for Trouncing the Competition"* by G. *Stalk, Jr. and R. Lachenauer, Harvard Business Review, April 2004* (11)

Both of these articles provide interesting perspectives on alternative strategies that are becoming increasingly important. The first addresses a non-traditional way to create and capture value – the open business model. The second takes a hard look at competitive strategies for the future.

Making Choices

Making your choice of strategies implies that you have defined several alternatives that could allow you to reach your Goals – alternatives ranging from improving your internal operations to changing your entire business. Before making your final choices, you need to understand the challenges that you are likely to face in implementing each different strategy.

Are those challenges minor or are they so great that your chances of success are minimal? That answer depends on the type and magnitude of change involved in a particular strategy. You also need to take a realistic look at the attractiveness of the businesses involved (particularly new businesses) and at how your business' strengths and weaknesses will come into play.

So first, we take a look at the **challenges**. Strategies involving minor modifications and evolutionary changes to your business will involve challenges that you already are dealing with – familiar territory. These are generally lower risk strategies. Strategies involving disruptive or revolutionary changes will take you into unfamiliar territory. These are generally higher risk but also may provide bigger rewards. In either case, typical factors that you need to consider and understand before making choices include:

- A different Competitive environment (new competitors, competitive counter-moves)
- New business requirements (business practices, geography…)
- New technologies
- Finding additional/new resources (cash, talent, capital, facilities)
- Risk (investments, timing, probability of returns)
- Changing your organization (new competencies needed)

The next area to consider before making your strategy choice is **business attractiveness**. Whether or not you are thinking about changing your business definition, it is important to understand the attractiveness of the kinds of businesses you either already have or are considering developing.

Figure 12 shows one way to take a "big picture" look at business attractiveness. This approach uses both your business position and the attractiveness of the industry to allow you to judge the attractiveness of your specific business opportunity. Depending on the "box" that a particular business falls within, the strategy varies from investing in that business to harvesting it.

Criteria for Industry Attractiveness can include: Size, Growth, Profitability, Pricing, Competition; and Social, Environmental, and Legal factors. Criteria for your Business Position include: Size, Growth, Share, Profitability, and Core Competencies.

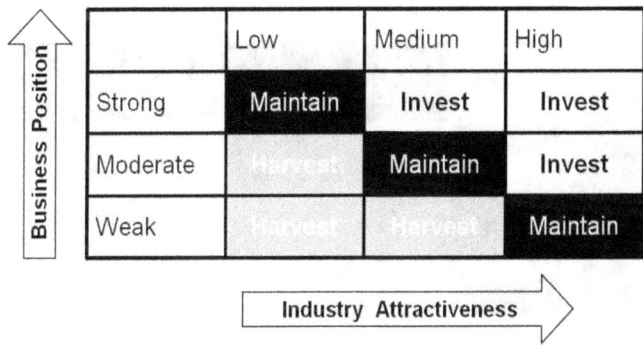

Figure 12: Business Attractiveness

Once you decide on suitable criteria, then you can place each business being considered in the appropriate box. For example, for a specific business, if the industry has low attractiveness and your business position is weak, continued or new investments in that business may not make sense. In other words, avoid or harvest that particular business. If, on the other hand businesses being considered fall in one of the boxes where the industry is attractive, investment in one of those businesses could be a good strategy. However, the strategy needs to be very different depending on the strength of your business position.

For more information on this kind of analysis, see the previously referenced book *"Competitive Strategy"* by M. Porter (Reference 6).

And finally, it is important to consider the **strengths and weaknesses** of your own business before choosing from among the alternative strategies. An accepted way to evaluate these strengths and weaknesses and to develop appropriate strategies around them is called a "SWOT" analysis. SWOT stands for Strengths, Weaknesses, Opportunities, and Threats. For a good but brief description of this technique see:

www.quickmba.com/strategy/swot (12).

SWOT Matrix	Strengths	Weaknesses
Opportunities	S-O Strategies	W-O Strategies
Threats	S-T Strategies	W-T Strategies

Figure 13: SWOT Analysis Matrix

Figure 13 shows the matrix that is commonly used in a SWOT analysis. The Baseline for your business (Step 1 of our process as described in Chapter 2) should provide you with most of the information you need for this kind of analysis. From your Internal Assessment you should have already identified your business Strengths and Weaknesses. From your External Assessment (Industry, Market, and Competitor analysis) you should be able to identify specific Opportunities and Threats.

Then the next step is to categorize the alternative strategies that you have developed: S-O Strategies (using your Strengths to address Opportunities), W-T strategies (strategies that address both your Weaknesses and key Threats), and so on. If you find that any of the boxes are empty, you may wish to consider additional strategies for that situation.

Doing this kind of analysis at this point in the business planning process accomplishes two things. First, it gives you a way to determine if you have developed a broad enough list of alternative strategies for consideration. And second, it challenges you to consider the seriousness of the vulnerabilities from your own internal weaknesses as well as external threats before you make your strategy choices.

And now is the time in this step of the planning process to make your strategy decisions. However if you would like some additional perspectives on making strategy choices, we suggest two articles: *"The Processes of Strategy Definition and Implementation"* by C. Christensen and J. Dann, *Harvard Business Review,* June 28, 1999 (13); and *"Scenario Planning: A Tool for Strategic Thinking"* by P. Schoemaker, *Sloan Management Review, Winter 1995* (14).

After making your choices, you should be able to list your key business strategies in order of importance. Now you are ready for the next step: Action Plans.

CHAPTER 4

ACTION PLANS (Step 5)

Now that you have determined your realistic business baseline, established achievable Goals, and chosen your key Strategies; the next step in our dynamic planning process (**Step 5**) is to develop specific plans for implementing those Strategies – plans that optimize the probability that you will achieve your Goals. These are what we call "Action Plans".

Looking at it from a different perspective, this planning process step is all about Programs and Priorities and defined Actions for carrying out those Programs – actions that are integrated and coordinated across your business with clear responsibilities assigned. More specifically, we have divided this step in our process into three parts:

- Selecting and Prioritizing Programs
- Developing Functional Plans
- Verifying Expected Outcomes

When you have finished this step (and this Chapter), you will understand how to create a detailed set of integrated Action Plans that can serve as your roadmap to future business success. You will know what will move you along your chosen path and who will do what along the way. You also will be reasonably sure that the path you have chosen provides you with a reasonable chance of reaching your destination.

PROGRAMS AND PRIORITIES

Selecting a strong portfolio of programs and establishing clear priorities among those programs is the first challenge in this step. In general, these programs will be either specific product development programs or "projects" associated with making, marketing, or supporting specific products.

But whatever the nature of the programs you are considering, there are numerous factors that need to be assessed before making your choices. These can be divided into two categories: risk factors and factors relating to importance/value.

The factors relating to risk determine how likely it is that the program will be successful – its probability of success. Risk Factors include attributes such as business fit, product competiveness, match with your core competencies, investment required, and resource availability. And each of these attributes has important "sub-attributes". For example, product competiveness includes factors such as cost, performance, and proprietary position. And resource availability includes things such as cash, capital equipment, and human resources with the right skill sets and talents.

The factors relating to importance/value address the overall importance of a program and its worth to your business. Importance/value factors include things such as strategic importance, size of the opportunity, expected returns, and time to expected returns.

Following are three examples of different ways to assess risk and importance/value. There are many other methods, but we thought that you might find one or more of these useful in making your program selections and establishing the priorities.

Figure 14 shows one way to evaluate program risk versus reward in order to determine "attractiveness". It addresses new products and compares program fit with your business (one aspect of risk) to one aspect of program value (attractiveness of the opportunity as determined by product innovation). For this comparison, it is important to factor your Core Competencies into "Business Fit" and to keep in mind that Innovation is from the CUSTOMERS' perspectives.

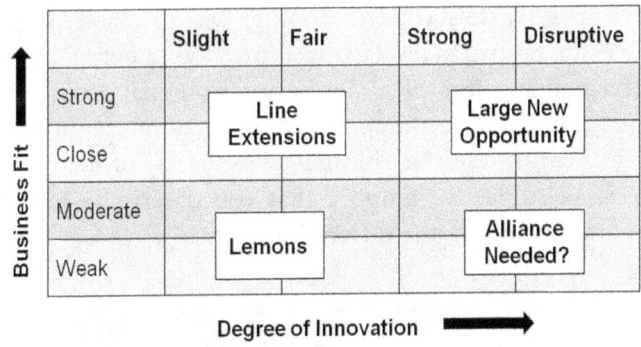

Figure 14: Program Risk versus Reward

From this type of analysis, you can judge the attractiveness of individual potential new products for YOUR business. For example, if your envisioned new product is already being sold by someone (no uniqueness) and its market is unrelated to those addressed by your business; this product is a "lemon" since your chance of business success is very low. On the other hand, if the potential product is highly innovative and fits directly into your business arena, it has significant potential. It presents a large, new opportunity for you where you have an excellent chance of being successful.

But the other two "boxes" shouldn't be discounted. If you already are a market leader and your Goal is to maintain your position or improve your profitability, then new products that are line extensions (minor modifications) can be valuable. However, they are unlikely to provide much growth. And if you have invented a potentially disruptive new product that fits outside of your business area, the growth potential is large – for someone. In this case an alliance or a licensing agreement may allow you to share in that opportunity. But beware of trying to pursue this "unrelated" new product on your own. It's not impossible to be successful, but it is very difficult when your core competencies are the "wrong" ones.

Figure 15 illustrates another way to assess program risk versus reward. This approach provides a comparison of the relative "values" of a number of potential programs. In this case, a program's expected return at some point in time (sales, profits, etc.) is plotted versus its probability of success (a subjective number that you determine based on the combination of the different risk factors).

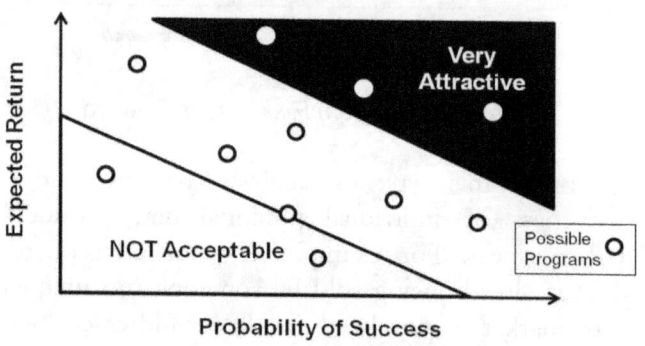

Figure 15: Program Value Comparison

If the expected return and the probability of success are both high, the program fits in the black triangle area – very attractive. Conversely, if the risk is high (probability of success is low) and the expected returns are low, the program falls into the lower left triangle area – not acceptable. And then there are those that fit "in-between" and may need a more in-depth assessment. You be the judge.

These are just two ways to compare programs, and neither considers important factors such as "time to returns" and "strategic importance". In other words, these kinds of analyses are useful but don't always provide enough information for decision-making. For a more in-depth look at evaluating new product programs, see the previously referenced book "*Winning at New Products*" by R. Cooper (Reference 3). In addition there are many other ways that you can discover for yourself with a little Internet searching (keywords like "product portfolio").

What we haven't addressed directly are the priorities. What Program is your business's top priority, what is next, and so on? **It is essential to establish clear Program priorities and to communicate them.** Some of the same techniques described above to select programs can also be used to prioritize them. However it is up to you to determine what is best for your business.

To provide additional insight into and help with determining priorities, you may find these two articles useful: "*Is It Real" Can We Win" Is It Worth Doing" (Managing Risk and Reward in an Innovation Portfolio)*" by G. Day, *Harvard Business Review*, December 2007 (15); and "*Decision Making: It's Not What You Think*" by H. Mintzberg and F. Westley, *Sloan Management Review*, Spring, 2001 (16). The first article describes a Real-Win-Worth analysis of programs. This is a more comprehensive approach to Program selection and prioritization than the specific techniques we have highlighted. The second article is about decision making, and describes different approaches that you might find useful.

Whatever techniques you use to choose and prioritize your programs, it is important to be sure that the programs selected are consistent with your strategies which in turn support your Goals. In other words, you need to verify that you do indeed have appropriate programs defined to support each key strategy and that collectively those programs will allow you to achieve your goals.

FUNCTIONAL PLANS

At this stage in our planning process, goals, strategies, programs and priorities have been established. Now it's time for planning appropriate actions (related to the Goals, Strategies, and Programs) by each business Function (Marketing and Sales, Manufacturing, Research and Development, Quality, Engineering, etc.) to carry out the programs. Without such actions there can be no business success. These Action Plans have several important requirements.

First is **consistency**. The planned actions of each Function must be consistent with the Goals, Strategies, and Priorities for the overall business. In other words, it is important for there to be one agreed upon set of business priorities. Then, it is essential for each Functional plan to be consistent with these priorities.

Next are the **programs**. Each Functional Plan must support the implementation of the same priority programs with resources, assigned responsibilities, and commitment to timelines and milestones.

And equally important is **coordination and integration**. No Function operates in isolation. Each is a critical element of the business. Therefore, for business success (achieving the Goals) it is essential that each Function's plans be integrated with the plans of the other Functions. In addition, each Function's actions must take into account the other Functions' constraints (skills, equipment, cash, etc.). Continuing communication and feedback among the Functions are required for achieving an effective level of integration. This is an iterative process that needs to be a coordinated business TEAM effort.

EXPECTED OUTCOMES

At this point, the business planning process is almost complete. However, before documenting and implementing your plan, it is important to re-test your chosen course. What are the expected outcomes? Will the portfolio of priority programs that you have selected and planned for achieve your goals if they are successful?

In other words, it's time to perform a new gap analysis to determine whether or not your proposed actions will take you to your desired arrival point (financial goals and business objectives), given your business constraints. More specifically, what are the projected results of your proposed plan? Are these results consistent with your goals, and is the investment exposure required to obtain these results acceptable?

A common way to assess expected financial outcomes of your proposed plan is to project sales and profits from your chosen priority programs and then compare the combined results to your financial goals. We recommend that you do this. However there are other considerations that also are important. Following we provide two examples of possible ways to visualize expected outcomes of your proposed plan. These techniques and other can help you assess its viability.

Figure 16 on the next page illustrates one type of financial projection of the evolution of a business. This analysis is based on the **collective** expected outcomes of planned programs. Plotted on the vertical axis is yearly ROCE (Return on Capital Employed) and on the horizontal axis is the yearly cash flow. This predicts how ROCE will evolve and in which year the business will transition from a negative cash flow situation to a positive cash flow based on the timing and the collective amounts of required investments for these programs.

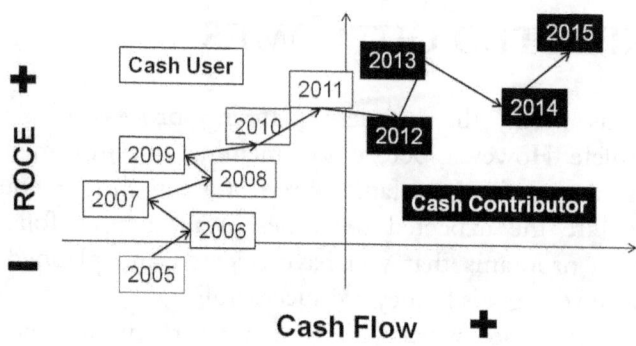

Figure 16: Expected Financial Performance

This way of looking at financial performance addresses the questions: Will your plan allow you to reach your ROCE goal? What will happen to cash flow if you proceed with the investments forecasted by your proposed business plan? Will you migrate from the cash user to the cash contributor zone in an acceptable timeframe? These questions are particularly important if there are finite reserves of cash or limited ability to borrow. In other words, this kind of plot is one way to determine if your proposed plan is financially acceptable and if you can afford to implement it.

Another important factor to consider for your proposed plan is the **risk/reward balance**. How risky is the new course? Do the potential rewards justify the risk? Can your business afford the level of risk?

Figure 17 exemplifies one type of risk/reward analysis for a proposed new course. On the vertical axis is the expected growth rate of your business based on your new plan. On the horizontal axis is the investment required to obtain that growth. Again, the data for this kind of plot come from the **collective** investments required and expected outcomes of your chosen priority programs.

Figure 17: Risk versus Reward

The lower left-hand box represents the case of few dollars being placed at risk to produce a moderate growth rate for the business. If this is where the projected outcome of your plan falls, you need to determine if this low growth rate is consistent with your business goals and objectives.

The top left-hand box represents the case that is almost "too good to be true" – a high growth rate achieved with minimum investment. If this is where the projected outcome of your plan falls you need to consider other types of risks to determine the probability that your plan will produce expected results. For example, if the growth potential is truly high and the barriers to entry are low, you are likely to face aggressive competitors. Do you have adequate competitive advantages to have an acceptable probability of winning?

The bottom right-hand box represents bad investments: a lot of risk for little return. It should be avoided. If this is where the expected outcome from your plan falls, you need to consider changing it.

The top, right-hand box is for the brave. There may be big rewards, but the risk is high. If the projected outcome of your plan falls here, you need to be sure that the level of financial risk is acceptable. And, before deciding to proceed, be sure to consider other risk factors that will impact your probability of success.

Once you are satisfied that you understand the expected outcome from your proposed plan, you have reached the point in the planning process where you (management) must decide whether or not to adopt the plan. If the expected outcome leads to the desired goals, within your business constraints (e.g., risk tolerance and availability of resources) – accept the plan. But it is important to identify the critical issues and key success factors that will impact whether or not you are successful.

However, if the expected outcome is unacceptable (given your business constraints), you need to either: revise your functional plans, revise your programs, revise your strategies (including reconsidering your business definition and/or your business model), and/or revise your goals. Then, look at the expected outcomes again. In other words, arriving at an actionable business plan is an iterative process: plan, test, revise and test again – until you are satisfied with the results.

Now, you should have verified that your plan does lead to your key goals, that you do have (or have access to) the resources needed for the plan (cash, capital, skills), and that there are no other business constraints that will prevent your plan from being successful. You are ready to document and implement your plan – the last two steps in our dynamic planning process.

CHAPTER 5

A BUSINESS PLAN DOCUMENT (Step 6)

At this point, if you have been following our process step-by-step, you should have all of the pieces of a business plan and have verified that together those pieces produce an acceptable outcome. Now it's time to produce a written document. This is **Step 6** in our process. But before starting to create your document, it's important to make sure that you do indeed have the necessary pieces:

- A realistic business Baseline (Step 1)
- Clear and specific Goals (Step 2)
- Well thought out Strategies (Steps 3 and 4)
- Detailed Action Plans, including Programs and Integrated Functional Plans (Step 5)

It is the sum of these pieces in written form that makes up your Business Plan **Document**. However which of these pieces you emphasize, how you format the document, how you write the text – it's up to you. There is no one best "template" for a business plan document. It is your challenge to use your specific pieces to create a compelling and convincing business guide that is appropriate for your unique set of circumstances – whether your business is just starting or is a large and complex established enterprise.

To create the right document, it is important to keep in mind its purpose. In Chapter 1, we highlighted the values of a Business Plan both as a sales tool and as a management tool. You may wish to review this because how you intend to use your plan has a strong influence on exactly what information your document should contain and how it should be presented.

However in this chapter we take a slightly different approach. We describe two basic business plan options – a streamlined plan (primarily for "internal" use) and a more detailed document (often required for influencing an "external" audience). We call the document with an internal focus the "Mini" Plan and the document with the external focus the "Complete" Plan.

THE "MINI" PLAN

The "Mini" Business Plan is our name for a document whose primary focus is internal. The primary value of such an internally focused business plan document is as a management tool. The audience is the business team and the emphasis is operational rather than descriptive. The uses for this type of plan are many:

- Clarifying strategies, determining objectives, influencing decisions
- Defining/prioritizing programs, allocating resources
- Establishing a baseline for business assessments and for tracking progress
- Providing a framework for evaluating new business opportunities and risks

- Communication & employee motivation

To summarize: The purpose of this kind of business plan document is to create and communicate the business framework to your entire team in a way that justifies and guides all activities and provides a "yardstick" by which to measure results and make needed "mid-course" corrections.

This kind of document doesn't need to contain detailed company, business, and/or market background information. However it should be specific enough to provide a clear perspective to your internal audience with respect to the key business plan elements (Goals, Strategies, Action Plans, and Financials). It also should provide enough information to justify the strategies and actions, and to convince your team that together you will be successful. This document should clearly answer questions such as: What is the current business situation? What are we going to do about it? What exactly do we intend to accomplish? Why will we be successful?

Although the format and contents are flexible, following is one outline for a "Mini" Business Plan document that you might find useful.

The "MINI" Business Plan

1. **Plan Summary**
   a. Business Definition and Description
   b. Financial Goals and Business Objectives
   c. Key Success Factors
2. **Status Assessment**
   a. Market and Competition Summary
   b. Business Summary
   c. Resources
3. **Strategy and Plans**
   a. Strategies and Rationale

      b. Programs and Priorities
      c. Functional Plans
      d. Milestones and Critical Issues

4. Financials
      a. Summary
      b. Current and Projected Performance, including key assumptions

Using an outline such as this will help you create a document that clearly and convincingly communicates the key elements of your plan (Baseline, Goals, Strategies, Action Plans) and provides the supporting financial information to your audience (your business team). Specifically, the Plan Summary establishes the business boundaries (existing or desired) and defines the goals and objectives. The Status Assessment provides the baseline for the plan. The Strategies & Plans and Financials sections are self-explanatory.

When the use for the plan is internal, this type of document is appropriate for most kinds of businesses, but the amount of information in each section can vary greatly depending on the complexity of the business. If the business is focused enough (e.g., a start-up business or one with a single product), it may be possible to condense this format by combining the first three sections into one – the Business Plan Summary. However, consider your situation carefully before jumping to this approach. This outline already represents a streamlined approach to a business plan document – what we consider the basic information needed to convince your business team to support your plan and for your plan to be useful as a management tool.

THE "COMPLETE" BUSINESS PLAN

An externally focused business plan is primarily a selling tool. Therefore it needs to be more detailed and complete than the Mini Plan – hence our name: "The Complete Business Plan".

The audience for an externally focused business plan is usually potential investors. That is obvious in the case of a typical start-up venture. But it is often the same for businesses (established or starting up) within larger companies. These businesses need the support of corporate management external to their specific businesses and therefore you must treat them as potential investors.

As mentioned above, one of the primary goals of this type of plan often is to obtain financing for developing or establishing a business, but there are other purposes as well. These include communicating with existing investors, gaining support for new courses of action, finding partners or establishing alliances, attracting key personnel, or even setting a value on you business.

Bottom line, the externally focused business plan must summarize what the business is and clearly demonstrate what it can be expected to do. It must convince the audience that the business is a good risk with strong potential.

To do this, the document must capture the attention of the audience, and it must be professional looking. It also must be complete and detailed, containing commonly expected information. And this information must be summarized appropriately with emphasis on the financials. And last but not least, the plan must be defensible, especially with respect to marketing. Although the contents of the Complete Business Plan can vary, the following basic format is a generally accepted one.

"Complete" Business Plan Basic Format

Cover Page
- Company name, address, contact information
- Confidentiality or other disclaimer

Plan Table of Contents
- Section and Subsection titles
- Page numbers included

Executive Summary
- Before or after the Table of Contents
- Can present a statement of purpose

Plan by Section
- Titles should be descriptive
- Order depends on the complexity and purpose of the plan

Appendix
- Resumes, brochures, literature
- Supplemental financial information
- Other relevant information, including key assumptions

This type of organization is what investors have come to expect. However the body of the plan (the Executive Summary and the Plan by Section) is the most important. Therefore we will take a look at this part in a little more detail.

The typical sections for the body of a complete business plan are: Executive Summary, Company Overview, Business Description, Market Analysis, Opportunity Identification, Strategies and Plans, Personnel Summary, and Financials.

Although the order may vary, together these sections should answer the five basic questions posed earlier and elaborated on below.

1. <u>Who are you and where are you now in the real world of business?</u> The answers to these questions are derived from your status assessments. This Baseline information

from Step 1 of our planning process is commonly presented in sections called Company Overview, Business Description, and Market Analysis.

2. <u>Where do you want to arrive, and when do you expect to get there?</u> The answers to these questions are the Financial Goals and Business Objectives from Step 2 of our planning process. These are highlighted in the Executive Summary and the Opportunity Identification sections.

3. <u>How are you going to get from where you are to where you want to be?</u> The answers are the Strategies, the Programs and the implementation and operational plans – the detailed Action Plans that will allow you to reach your Goals. This information (from Steps 4 and 5 of our planning process) is presented in detail in the Strategies & Plans section.

4. <u>What is your current financial picture and what will it be – if you follow your plan?</u> In a literal sense, the answers to these questions are the "bottom line." Summaries of financial information can be found in a various sections (Executive Summary and Business Description being the most common), but the complete picture is provided in the Financials Section.

5. <u>How will you execute your plan?</u> This typically means what are the sources and uses of funds and other resources? The complete answers to these questions are usually found in the Personnel Summary and the Financials sections. However a summary of parts of this may be provided in the Strategies and Plans section.

With this as background, let's take a look at the rationale for each section in more detail.

Executive Summary.

Usually potential investors read the Executive Summary first. If they are interested, then they read some or all of the details of the rest of the plan. Therefore, the Executive Summary should to be viewed as the "entrance gate" and should clearly **summarize** the answers to the questions: Who are you? Where do you want to arrive? Why will you be successful? What do you need? Bottom line: Why is investing in your company a good business proposition?

In other words, the Executive Summary is a "sales pitch." Investors have many possible choices. You need to convincingly explain why they should choose investing in your business over others. Remember that any investment stems from a "risk-reward" decision. It is important to be honest about the risks but it is acceptable to highlight not only the EXPECTED rewards, but also the POSSIBLE rewards, even if they are not the most likely outcomes. And today, it is particularly important to stress the uniqueness of your business opportunity and any other factors that will shield it from an economic downturn.

Although the Executive Summary does not need to be a complete summary of the Business plan, it should address in some fashion each of the main areas. Typical contents of an Executive Summary include:

- Company Description/Business Overview
- Business Objectives
- Market Opportunity & Strategies for addressing
- Financial goals & projections
- Financing & other needs
- Key Success Factors

However, keep in mind that potential investors are usually most interested in your specific financial opportunity, the strengths and unique factors that will allow your business to successfully capture this opportunity, and your specific needs to be successful (financial or others).

Concise summaries of these key elements, presented in a compelling manner, will go a long way towards interesting potential investors and even gaining support for your plan from your own business team. The details of the plan and its justification are best left to the other sections of the document.

From this point on, the plan document needs to be detailed and specific. However each of the remaining sections can start with a summary if desired.

Company Overview

The Company Overview section is just what the title implies – a look at the company basics. Typical Contents include:

- Company Legal Structure, Ownership, Locations(s)
- History or Start-up Plan
- Strategic Partners
- Staffing
- Equipment, Facilities, other Assets
- Liabilities and Debts
- Core Competencies and Intellectual Property

Although this may seem like just background material, it does contain some particularly important information: the resources currently available (including cash and human resource skill sets), your Core Competencies, and your Intellectual Property.

Business Description

The Business Description section tells your audience what business you are in, how you operate (suppliers, sourcing, distribution, etc.), what your products are. It identifies your customers and main competitors, and explains your company's competitive advantage over other companies operating in the same business segment. Typical contents of this section include:

- Current Business Definition & Business Model
- Current products and unique advantages
- Customer benefits and needs addressed
- Competitors & Competitive Products
- Organization & Operations
- Significant accomplishments, financial performance

This section also should summarize the overall health of the business – sales and profits, growth, other significant accomplishments. If necessary, the present situation can be analyzed by dividing the business into various components, such as major products lines.

Areas often covered include product quality, the manufacturing situation (both internally manufactured and outsourced products), manufacturing costs in relation to market prices, and distribution channels and their costs.

Market Analysis

The typical contents of the Market Analysis section include:

- Industry description, trends & principal players
- Market segments (geography, size, growth, trends)
- Customer description & their unmet needs
- Distribution patterns
- Competition (direct, indirect, future)
- Barriers to entry
- Key success factors

Specifically, you should provide the trends and growth rates for each segment, the criteria for winning, and a comparison of your business' strengths and weaknesses with those of your competitors. In other words, this section contains data relative to market size, its global nature, and how it is changing. It identifies current and potential competitors and provides data related to their performance (along with similar data for your company). Business strategies and business models for all players should be covered and an analysis provided of their strengths and weaknesses.

Questions you may wish to address include: What is the marketing strategy for your company or business? Do you have a competitive edge? If so, what is it? What is your pricing strategy versus your competitors? How do your sales and promotion strategies differ from those of your competitors?

Opportunity Identification

To summarize, this section is a complete description of the business opportunity/path you intend to pursue. Typical contents include:

- Target market segments
- Opportunity description
- Your strengths & weaknesses versus competition
- Financial Goals & Business Objectives
- Risks and key success factors
- Business constraints

Any competitive advantage that you have with respect to the market you target should be detailed here. You should be answering questions such as: Is your company "ahead of the curve" with respect to the market trends? Is your company better positioned than the competition to compete in the intended markets? Again, this section should include appropriate data and their analysis.

Note: The information in this section is sometimes included with strategies and plans. However often it is important enough to be detailed in a separate section such as this.

Strategies and Plans

In the Strategies & Plans section, you should describe in detail how you plan to get from where you are to the Goals you have set, and you need to identify who will do what. Typical contents of this section include:

- Business strategies, value propositions
- Marketing & sales strategies, competitive positioning
- Product strategies & programs, timelines, milestones
- Functional plans
- Resources/investments needed
- Expected outcomes & critical issues

Whether you plan to expand your business definition, adopt a new business model, develop new products, make acquisitions, or take some other action, this is where you show how and why you can win. You need to emphasize **what** you plan to change, **how**, and **when**.

Each type of change needs to be described, including: fundamental strategy shifts or new strategies, expansion of the markets served or new markets to be addressed, changes in your product lines or proposed new products, and/or management or organizational changes.

And this is the section where you describe and justify in detail (with data) the resources/investments needed to carry out your plan. You must either verify that the resources needed are within current capabilities or describe the plan to obtain them. If you are seeking additional funds because the surrounding competitive scenario has changed, then a thorough analysis of the new and old competitive situation is usually adequate to justify the request for additional funds. However if you are proposing a new endeavor, potential investors are likely to want more information.

Additionally it is important to identify key issues and describe how each will be addressed. These could include value proposition, resource gaps, organizational barriers, etc. Also important is an assessment of the probability that the critical issues can be resolved and that the plan can be successful in the time frame defined.

Personnel Summary

The content of the Personnel Summary section is pretty straightforward and typically includes:

- Organizational structure
- Key Management personnel
- Human resources & skill sets
- Professional resources
- Gaps & critical issues
- Personnel plan

However one area needs special attention – skill sets. Often key skills sets are missing in start-up ventures or businesses making "radical" changes in direction. These gaps should be identified and filling them should be addressed specifically. Sometimes businesses choose to purchase needed skill sets or support from the "outside". This can include professional resources such as consultants, attorneys, CPA's, or other kinds of support personnel. If this is the plan, it should be noted. In addition, if some specialized skill is needed (e.g., a particular type of consultant), that should be highlighted.

Financials

Numbers and more numbers and details. That's what this section contains. Typical contents include:

- Summary & projections of key financial indicators
- Sources & use of funds
- Historical & current financial performance
- Detailed financial projections
- Projected business ratios
- Key assumptions and critical issues

The emphasis in this section is on the actual financial picture and how it will change with the new/modified plan. Therefore, although some of this information may be summarized in other parts of the plan, this section should include detailed financial data for the overall company/business for the past (3 to 5 years is common) and for the current period. It should also present future financial projections (usually 5 years).

Any unusual situations should be indicated, and any important assumptions should be identified. The data presented usually include things such as break-even and cash flow analyses, profit and loss statements, and the balance sheet.

It is important to keep in mind that the analysis of the past/current financials of your business is necessary to provide credibility for what you want to do next. As far as your future projections are concerned, it is helpful to present three cases: expected results if nothing is changed (worst case), expected results if the new plan is funded and successful (most likely), and best possible results (best case). This then provides justification for supporting the plan you have developed.

SUMMARY

To summarize, whatever the focus, the essential elements of the "Mini" Business Plan and the "Complete" Business Plan are the same – the Baseline, Goals, Strategies, Action Plans, and supporting financial information. And whatever format and level of detail you choose, this is the kind of information that needs to be clearly documented and put in the context of your current business to gain the support needed for implementing your plan.

If you would like to look at some business plan examples, searching on the internet is a good way to start. The key words "Business Plan" will yield many relevant results. One site we recommend is the Small Business Administration's site:

www.sba.gov/ smallbusinessplanner/ plan/ writeabusinessplan / SERV_WRRITINGBUSPLAN.html (17)

If you would like a book with more complete descriptions of the various sections of a business plan (or a different perspective on the document), Amazon.com offers many choices. One that has a good section on financing is:

"The Ernst & Young Business Plan Guide" by B. Ford, J. Bornstein, and P. Pruitt, John Wiley a& Sons, 2007 (18)

If you would like software to help you document your plan, there are many packages available. One that we have found useful is PaloAlto Software's *"Business Plan Pro"*:

www.bplans.com/ business_plan_software (19)

CONCLUSION

THE "LIVING" BUSINESS PLAN (Step 7)

At this point, you should have in hand the knowledge to create a compelling, written guide to your business future – Your Business Plan.

The next challenge is to execute that plan in a way that it becomes a living document, evolving as your business world changes. Creating this "living" business plan is **Step 7**, the final step in our business planning process. It is a key to your future business success.

Why do you need a living business plan? To paraphrase from Chapter 1 (Pitfall 4, lack of mid-course corrections):

> "New competitors are being born, customer requirements evolve, technology advances, the economy changes, and so on. To be relevant in this dynamic business environment, your plan also needs to be dynamic. Aiming toward a Goal with a "fixed" plan is like trying to drive a car without steering. At best you are likely to end up at an unexpected destination. At the worst, you will drive off a cliff."

Disasters caused by plan obsolescence can be avoided by adopting a cyclic process to create a "living" business plan. Simply this process consists of four stages: execute the plan, monitor the results, take corrective action, and repeat the process. These actions are described below and together make up the final step in our planning process.

EXECUTE THE PLAN

The first step towards breathing life into your business plan is execution of that plan. Executing a business plan is every bit as challenging as creating the plan, and is just as critical. This complicated and sometimes controversial topic is covered in depth by many books and papers, a number of which focus on the "the management of change".

Because of its importance and complexity, we feel that doing justice to this aspect of business planning is beyond the scope of this book on basics. However, we do provide a few words of explanation about areas that generally are considered the **key success factors** for successful plan implementation. Although some of these have been touched on in other chapters, we bring them together here for emphasis.

Funding/Support

Without adequate funding and appropriate support, your plan and your business are doomed to failure. Gaining these comes down to your ability to "sell" your plan to the appropriate audience. This comes down to creating a compelling document and presenting it in a convincing way.

Leadership

An effective leader is essential for the success of almost any team endeavor, and implementation of a business plan is certainly a "team sport". Although there are many attributes that contribute to effective leadership, in the case of business plan implementation providing consistent direction and making sure messages are unambiguous are keys.

Communication

This starts with clear DOWNWARD communication of the key elements of the plan to the entire organization. But that is only the beginning. There needs to be: rapid and complete SIDEWAYS communication across the organization to keep actions coordinated, clear UPWARD communication related to decision-making and progress/obstacles, and appropriate sharing of information both inside and outside of the organization with people having a need-to-know.

Responsibilities

All employees must have clearly assigned responsibilities and expectations. However it is equally important to clarify to the entire organization who has responsibility for making what decisions.

Motivation

Presenting a compelling case for the Business Plan is a part of motivating employees and gaining their support. However, understanding by each employee of the business implications of their daily decisions is even more important.

Organization

Often leaders focus on restructuring as the solution to business plan execution. Having the right organization is important, but the other key success factors are just as important – and sometimes they are even more important.

For a more in-depth look at issues and suggested approaches for executing a new plan and change management, use the key words "organizational change" and either generally search the Web or look for books and articles at amazon.com. In addition, two articles that you may find useful are:

> *"Leadership in a Combat Zone"* by W. Pagonis,
> Harvard Business Review, December 2001 (20)

> *"The Secrets to Successful Strategy Execution"* by G.
> Neilson, K. Martin, and E. Powers, Harvard
> Business Review, June 2008 (21)

They provide various perspectives on and examples of making change happen.

MONITOR THE RESULTS

The second step in the cycle of the "living" business plan is Monitoring Results. To do this, you must create and use a process to track actual results and then compare them to "expected results" from your plan. This is essential in order to identify the needed corrective actions and/or plan revisions to keep your organization aimed at your Goals.

The areas that commonly need **periodic review** include:

- Milestones – the ones you should have established before starting plan implementation
- Key performance measures (often financial)
- Programs and their progress
- Product portfolio changes
- Plan expected results

However, it is up to you to pick the appropriate specific focus areas and then create the review process by: determining the appropriate review frequency, identifying the reviewers, establishing the review format, and specifying the data to be presented and compared to the targets for the particular area being reviewed. We strongly suggest that you consider monthly reviews for areas that are key or particularly dynamic and quarterly reviews for the others.

We also suggest that you create a simple, graphic way of showing progress/results versus expectations and identifying critical issues. A color-coded template based on an Excel spreadsheet can serve as this kind of an updatable "dashboard".

What are some of the typical issues that arise during Business Plan execution?

- Programs behind schedule
- Shortage of cash or other resources
- Inadequate manufacturing equipment
- High product cost and/or poor product quality
- Poor financial results compared to expectations

Your monitoring process should enable you not only to identify these types of issues, but also to determine the root causes of the problems (deviation analysis). With this information in hand, you can proceed to the next step in the cycle – taking corrective action.

CORRECTIVE ACTION

Making revisions (taking corrective action) is the final step in the cycle of the "living" business plan. These revisions fall into two categories: mid-course corrections and Business Plan changes. Based on your monitoring results, you should be able to determine which of these kinds of revisions you need.

Typically mid-course corrections address organizational issues such as project management skills, lack of effective prioritization, and productivity. These kinds of changes do not necessarily require significant business plan revision to correct.

However, unanticipated obstacles often do require updating/revising the business plan or sometimes even abandoning the old plan and developing a new one. Examples of these types of issues include incorrect forecasting of costs and/or capabilities, unanticipated competition or market change, pressure from external forces (e.g., a downturn in the economy), or insurmountable obstacles such as technology inadequacy or major program timing miscalculations.

Once you have completed this final stage in Step 7 of our business planning process, you are ready to continue implementing a "living" business plan.

CLOSING THOUGHTS

We hope that this basic guide has provided you with a useful perspective on the business planning process, and has convinced you of the importance of creating and executing a compelling and living Business Plan.

If so, you are ready to navigate today's sea of economic chaos to business success in tomorrow's disruptive environment.

Management Guidance
for Disruptive Times

REFERENCES

_____

CHAPTER 2

1. A more detailed look at the concept of business definition:
   www.12manage.com/methods_abell_three_dimensional_busi ness_definition.html
2. A description of the concept of "Business Model," along with examples:
   en.wikipedia.org/wiki/Business_model
3. Additional information related to product assessments:
   "Winning at New Products" by R.G. Cooper, Perseus Publishing, 2001
4. Additional insight into internal assessment:
   "How to Appraise Your Organization Capabilities and Disabilities" by C. Christensen, Harvard Business Review, June 11, 1997
5. A summary of "Porter's 5 Forces Model for Industry Analysis":
   www.quickmba.com/strategy/porter.shtml
6. THE classic text on industry/market analysis:
   "Competitive Strategy, Techniques for Analyzing Industries and Competitors" by Michael Porter, The Free Press (Simon & Schuster), 1980

7. A good summary on competitive analysis and sources of information:
   www.sba.gov/smallbusinessplanner/manage/marketandprice/SERV_COMPANAYLSIS.html

CHAPTER 3

8. Additional information on common risks associated with external forces:
   "Countering the Biggest Risk of All" by A. Slywotzky and J. Drzik, Harvard Business Review, April 2005.
9. An understandable article that starts from a modification of Porter's 5 Forces model and explores game-changing actions:
   "The Right Game: Use Game Theory to Shape Strategy" by A. Brandenburger and B. Nalebuff, Harvard Business Review, July-August 1995
10. Addresses a non-traditional way to create and capture value:
    "Why Companies Should Have Open Business Models" by H. Chesbrough, MITSloan Management Review, Winter 2007
11. A hard look at competitive strategies for the future:
    "Hardball: Five Killer Strategies for Trouncing the Competition" by G. Stalk, Jr. and R. Lachenauer, Harvard Business Review, April 2004
12. A good but brief description of SWOT analysis:
    www.quickmba.com/strategy/swot
13. Making strategy choices:
    "The Processes of Strategy Definition and Implementation" by C. Christensen and J. Dann, Harvard Business Review, June 28, 1999
14. Making strategy choices:
    "Scenario Planning: A Tool for Strategic Thinking" by P. Schoemaker, Sloan Management Review, Winter 1995

CHAPTER 4

15. A comprehensive approach to Program selection and prioritization:
    "Is It Real? Can We Win? Is It Worth Doing? (Managing Risk and Reward in an Innovation Portfolio)" by G. Day, Harvard Business Review, December 2007
16. Different approaches to decision making:
    "Decision Making: It's Not What You Think" by H. Mintzberg and F. Westley, Sloan Management Review, Spring, 2001

CHAPTER 5

17. Basic business plan information and examples:
    www.sba.gov/smallbusinessplanner/plan/writeabusinessplan/SERV_WRRITINGBUSPLAN.html
18. For more complete descriptions of the various sections of a business plan:
    "The Ernst & Young Business Plan Guide" by B. Ford, J. Bornstein, and P. Pruitt, John Wiley & Sons, 2007
19. Software to help document your plan:
    www.bplans.com/business_plan_software

CONCLUSION

20. *"Leadership in a Combat Zone"* by W. Pagonis, Harvard Business Review, December 2001
21. *"The Secrets to Successful Strategy Execution"* by G. Neilson, K. Martin, and E. Powers, Harvard Business Review, June 2008

ABOUT THE AUTHORS

Dr. Carol Fatuzzo is the founder, President, and CEO of New Horizons Business Ventures, Inc. (NHBV). Prior to founding NHBV, Dr. Fatuzzo served as a Technical Director for 3M, one of the 100 largest US Manufacturing Corporations. Dr. Fatuzzo's professional career includes over 30 years of technical and leadership positions in a variety of global businesses. For more information about Dr. C. Fatuzzo, visit her Website: **nhbvinc.com**.

Dr. Ennio Fatuzzo is the President and CEO of EF Management Associates, Inc (EFMA). He is a seasoned corporate executive with extensive experience in managing large organizations, combating external business threats, and building synergy through acquisitions. Prior to EFMA, Dr. Fatuzzo founded and led AIM, Inc., an international business consulting company, and held business executive positions in 3M and other global enterprises. For more information about Dr. E. Fatuzzo, visit his Website: **efmainc.com**.

www.ingramcontent.com/pod-product-compliance
Lightning Source LLC
Chambersburg PA
CBHW071237170526
45165CB00003B/1131